APHORISMS & ESSAYS

Tania Peitzker

"Acceptance is a scalable virtue"

Tania Peitzker, Technologist & Educator
St Rita de Cascia Church, Nice, Côte d'Azur, *2019.*

"Grant me COFFEE [courage] to change the things I can

Grant me WINE to accept the things I can't [change]"

Anonymous Wall Decoration, Riff on Niebuhr's "Serenity Prayer"
Blue Lady Pub, Australia/Invasion Day, Antibes, 2019.

Dedicated to my family & friends
in England, Australia, Germany, Switzerland, France, Italy,
the USA & Canada.

Publishing this ebook today is to show that some things cannot be done by algorithms: creative writers are indeed forever safe from Artificial Intelligence – as currently defined!

Gilets Jaunes on Garibaldi Place

Tania Peitzker

Traditional Fishing Boats of Nissa

Monaco

APHORISMS: Part I

Any problem can be solved

if you change the way you think about it.

If love is a lemon

then make lemonade

just make sure you get the right amounts of

sugar and water.

Computer work can make you blind

to the living breathing realities around you

Creativity leads to bliss

in a world made smaller by mean spirits

to fight for closure

is the most noble battle of all

Know thyself and become the stronger person. Love thyself and be the better one.

Withhold your love

till you are sure of

at least the intention

to respect it

ESSAY 1: The Future

I deal in futures. Futurities. Not the stock market though my technology company in Artificial Intelligence will be listing on the Frankfurt Stock Exchange in ca 24 months. A future 5 year plan that looks forward to Emerging Tech finally arriving.

Many people are now calling themselves "Futurists" or speculative thinkers on the future of society. Because of technology and perceived threats. There are certainly downsides to some tech – social media's malignant ability to disseminate harmful material is just one case in point.

I could be a Futurist as well. Reading HG Wells "The Time Machine" makes me think that Science Fiction is an easy domain to live in. Granted it is largely inhabited by males in the present and I wonder why they are overwhelmingly keen to indulge all their free time in sci fi speculations and repetitive fantasies of perfect miniature anime girlfriends like Weena and the Asian versions with Manga fantasy females.

The present day geeks imagine futuristically triumphing over troll-like beings in their weedy nerdy forms. As in gaming, computer games that have an addictive hold on many of their escapist minds now.

The future is bright in that more women and girls are entering it with technological skills. Then the alarming news hits: the number of women employed in the tech industry HAS SUNK to 1980s levels.

Females now number less than 20% of the high tech workforce. How could that have happened? With all the Computer Science grads, Engineering women students and STEM policies pushing girls to take up scientific subjects in earnest at tertiary level?

It has sneaked up on us. The Anti Women Tech Backlash. Here we were convinced by the increasing numbers of women and girls in STEM industries and even in management, even founding tech companies and WHAM. Back to the Dark Ages of the men do math, women do the nurturing and child-rearing. Family support stuff.

To write this essay on the future, I tried really hard to find a BBC article I saw a few months ago. It summarised the best 7 positive developments of mankind over the last century. So we could take a break from the Bad News stories and try to rest our minds in the knowledge that the future will take care of things.

We are a smart race, we'll figure it out before we consign our species to apocalyptic devastation of the suicidal mental illness and environmental devastation of the Climate Change kind.

And the article has disappeared. Have searched for it and keep finding Old Good News stories from a few years ago. Numerous TED speakers posing as liberals but from the Trumpian New Right no doubt, convincing us we have less chance of being murdered, getting a terminal illness, being run over, starving, poverty, homeless, lonely etc.

It doesn't ring true. We see homelessness and poverty rates tripling in the United Kingdom over the past few years. I describe all that in my second essay in this volume: The Past as it is what Great Britain evidently is entrenched in.

Nostalgic fantasies of its past Greatness when Britain could rule the world without much conscience nagging about suppressing other people, violent invasions and even more brutal slamming down of uprisings and mental subversion.

The future indubitably has helped the Third World countries edge closer to the living standards of the First World. That can only be a good thing. But what have we subjected them to in the process?

We being the controllers of the Internet (the US military largely controls the Web to be precise, a fact we all pretend to forget). The Masters of Fossil Fuel infrastructure that must at all cost be replaced by renewably powered machinery, equipment and technology.

No wonder there is a present and future clash of resources and global development. India and African nations, poor Asian countries and the Continent of South America are all determined to "catch up" with our European and North American Quality of Life. It is what they now see daily on their phones in a dusty village with little water, squatting scared of militia but dreaming of skyscrapers and chain store living that is broadcast into their pockets.

Fast Moving Consumer Goods are tracking their way to the African continent, courtesy of Amazon delivery drones or Google Maps or Instagram photoshopped marketing of easily achievable glamour and luxury. You too can have it all when in the West the masses are now rising up to say Hey where is my fair share?

Facebook drives the future of want. The need to connect on Twitter. The invasive sharing of private moments on SnapChat, making the young wherever they are susceptible and indescribably vulnerable to predatory people, exploitative practices and harmful thoughts.

Evil is an old fashioned concept yet it manifests in disgusting ways on the invisible web connecting us all: telling girls they must be ashamed of themselves, nobody is good enough, young people must be anxious for their futures, they should be pressured into feeling inadequate, needy and end up for all this torrent of "communication" being isolated and the loneliest people our history has ever known.

The "self harm" manifestations of the evil side of the Net are now getting public notice and some politicians are dutifully shouting to ban social media, the tech giants who miraculously can make billion dollar turnover a year, pay very little corporate tax back into the societies they are mining for their lucrative data streams, and yet are not in the position to eradicate online material telling vulnerable children and adults to kill themselves, mutilate their bodies and weaken their minds with anxieties and fear.

Corporate ethics is now one of the futuristic subjects in my industry. Artificially intelligent algorithms might get out of control, robots could turn on us, humans lose their mastery of the physical universe. It is a subject that needs to be brought back into the present because that is where the harm is being done, right now to the people all around us, in every country in the world.

The United Nations and Amnesty published startling statistics not long ago that I am trying to promulgate, though I am then looked upon as a doomsayer and alarmist. Much like trying to push people to combine Greentech, AI and climate change action.

Who cares? "Not my field of expertise" says an AI "thought leader" though her hometown of Sydney is becoming repeatedly uninhabitable in the onslought of dust storms, unbearable heatwaves of 44 degrees killing the young, old and ill, lack of water and rivers so toxic and dry that millions of fish are now floating dead in them.

2019 is fin de siecle year, looking ahead to the next decade, our 5 year plan included. I can put the Tech Hat on and be glad that I am one of the Global Elite. I am OK, am in the world's Top 5 ranking for AI companies founded by women; in the top 3 of NLP ventures founded by women in Europe. Why should I care?

Because the UN report said that over 2/3 of women and girls surveyed globally said they had experienced violence and abuse on the internet. That is why I care. That is unacceptable and must be changed by all of us right now in the present. The future will not just take care of itself.

APHORISMS: Part II

Love is a self-deluded gift of torture

able to delight and pain

in equal measure

transport yourself
with higher thoughts

bigger things than

a tiny human ego

if we cared for one another

as narcissists do for themselves

the world would shine

with unbroken love

healing from narcissistic

attacks takes time

recovery depends on

recognition of ill will

When women achieve less than men in the public domain,

it is not for the lack of works, but for the want of publicity

and permanent recognition

I don't believe in conspiracies but there are sure as hell

a lot of people who like to undermine that which threatens them

ESSAY 2: The Past

They say writing is a form of therapy. In fact it has been medically proven that it helps with overcoming "emotional trauma" and eases depression. I do it because I love it and people tell me how much they enjoy my writing style. My high school teachers were convinced I was going to be a "Great Australian Writer" and I did aspire to becoming the next Patrick White.

He seems like an old fogey now to me, looking back on the past 30 years since I left school in Far North Tropical Queensland. Cairns was a delightful place to grow up for children, full of adventures as well as poisonous deadly snakes, jellyfish, sharks, stingrays, deadly spiders, insects and toxic cane toads, not to mention the flora with stinging bushes and falling trees. Yet I survived running through the bush and sailing on crocodile-infested seas, somehow. As the Aussies say, with a lot of good luck.

Now the the threat, surfacing from decades of environmental damage and global climate devastation, is skin cancer caused by the sunshine. The one element that Australians believe is not out to get them, though monstrous cyclones and flooding storms may do their worst. The 2018-19 drought is something they can't deny now. With January the hottest month in their history, it cannot be ignored. Heatwaves are killing people right in the middle of the sophisticated high tech cities, not just in the Outback.

So the past of lies, ignorance, denials and blockading of climate change action is finally catching up with Australians. As it is with Americans who are unable to take deep breaths outdoors because they could die in an instant by freezing their lungs. The Siberian – 44 degrees, the exact Polar opposite to the lethal heat Down Under, is causing frostbite to faces and fingers by stepping outdoors in Chicago and the Great Lakes.

Again, American denial of climate change and clinging to fossil fuels has come back to bite them on the bum, as an Australian would describe it. Will they change? Will they deal with the past errors and missed opportunities? Can they please finally wholeheartedly embrace the URGENT ACTION required to avoid the ending of the planet as we know it ie an inhabitable and enjoyable one shared with respect for other species, flora and fauna, animals and plants?

Australian schoolchildren have gone on strike and no doubt will do so again this year, regardless of Right Wing authorities tell them to do. I picked up DIE ZEIT yesterday in the Nice State Library and the cover story was about a young Swedish girl who is on permanent strike about Global Warming and leading an online campaign among her peers internationally. From the mouth of babes come the warrior words of tomorrow and today.

The Past is an example of how we live through trauma, grief and mistakes and then we recollect them in the present. We leave it haplessly to our future to sort out a lot of this stuff. It won't happen this time round, that is why we need the Paris Accord actioned and not sanctioned. That is why when I read today that a leading Tory Member of Parliament, in all the Brexit chaos, has succeeded in pocketing nearly a million dollars in bribes from Greentech companies that will benefit from his influence on the UK Climate Change Committee.

Even the leaders we elect to do something about it can't get on with the job and align their professed concern with morals and action to secure our futures. No wonder there is a mistrust in governments around the world. These elected reps keep doing us over. Why should we trust meglo-maniacs and narcissists who unfortunately keep popping up in positions of influence, power and trust?

I wanted to explore the past five years I have endured in Brexit Britain here. Yet that may be a subject for a novella as the various English traumas I endured socially, professionally and politically will take time to heal. The Brits, I have discovered, have a very special way of exercising their Superiority Complex, a leftover from Empire Days.

Sadly their class consciousness permeates all classes, even the working classes feel superior to the migrants, the migrants superior to the refugees, the housed refugees to the homeless Brits, addicts, alcoholics and more and more, the mentally ill. The mentally disturbed people of Britain are on the rise and have nowhere to go: their infrastructure is completely inadequate and unable to deal with the growing numbers of ordinary people just suddenly breaking down.

It is a matter of contempt for others deeply held in a society if those in power, in the authorities, in charge of budgets and the distribution of taxpayer money, cannot and will not accept the facts facing them. The miserable, appalling outcomes of Austerity and the cutbacks in hospital and policing staff. It is even driving those staff over the edge.

I have never lived in such a hypocritical society, where the Government and Departments tell honest surgeons, doctors and nurses that they are lying about their hospitals not being fit for purpose.

That the medics should not close their wards because they will cause more harm open than trying to care for patients without the adequate staff numbers, equipment and money. In many parts of Great Britain, you may be safer in a war zone where you know at least the Doctors Without Borders and the United Nations have set up functioning Red Cross hospitals.

It has become hit and miss in England. I know that the Scots know this is the case which is why they want out, they want to be free of this superiority-driven, deceitful and endlessly chaotic mess. The Welsh are generally a kind and peaceful people, I think they are incensed by the English litany of lies and incompetence. Snouts in the trough and on a jolly are two ways to describe the current state of affairs.

Xenophobia is a problem in most countries these days, surfacing from their various pasts, colonial or otherwise. Dealing with one's own history is never easy, let alone confronting the worst elements of one's country's history.

Australia has never done that on Aboriginal relations effectively. It is the only country not to have a treaty with the First or Indigenous Peoples. They must take a lesson from the history book of Germany: their dedicated, continual *Auseinandersetzung* with genocide and hate speech, the dark side of humanity ever present, everywhere.

The UK "national discourse" is very often obsessed with hating or at least frequently sneering, denigrating and despising Germany, which many Germans remain entirely oblivious to. Many classes in British society hold onto their winning World War II as a safety blanket, they will be winners again, without ever addressing their colonial legacy of violence in India, Africa and other places.

The BBC, to its eternal shame, continually promotes these sentiments: they rarely cover any positive news in Germany and most English people know very little about the country apart from their pre 1950s notions of the place, fed to them in vintage collectible items from posters to clothings to personal memorabilia of "being at war".

It was no surprise then that the Prime Minister Theresa May called her group of advisers on Brexit "The War Cabinet". The daily media headlines for over two years now harp on about the "UK being at war with Brussels" and that the "Europeans are out to get them". Above all, their favourite, standard anti-Teutonic trope is that "Germany is trying to punish Britain".

May's humdinger for all posterity will be her revival of Adolf Hitler's speech hating "the global elite". She paraphrased how cosmopolitan mobile workers of today are "citizens of nowhere". Disparaging them as some sort of rootless, parasitic tribe.

Never minding the fact they are vital to the global economy, to the British wellbeing past and future and above all the survival of London. No wonder the Laborite London Mayor quickly tried to declare a future Republic of London!

Yet May's "create a hostile environment" to discourage all migrant workers, refugees and the highly skilled alike, remains with her Home Office mission and War Cabinet objectives. The hostility experienced by City Workers and farmhands alike is unspeakable and will be a matter of national shame for decades to come.

That's if the British public and their leaders ever truly undertake an Auseinandersetzung that has led to outbreaks of pedophilila like the Jimmy Saville and Rochedale cases involving 1000s of young victims known to the British authorities *for decades* and cover ups like Grenfell Tower where warnings were given, repeated and ignored.

When their former Foreign Minister and London Mayor Boris Johnson, now with laughable aspirations to being a Churchillian PM in the near future, comes out with extremist descriptives like "The EU is Hitler's plan completed" and that "The Germans are punishing Britons like in a concentration camp", then you know the society is in trouble.

To top it off, Mr Johnson also exploded when confronted by journalists saying that businesses and big companies in his country are paralysed and losing loads of money, due to his cohort's Brexit prevarications and grossly incompetent administration.

He retorted simply *"Fuck Business"* and one can understand why London is a seething mess of broken transport, overpriced real estate, money laundering, sex trafficking and officially the title holder of Most Polluted City in Europe.

I write this here not to be polemical about the recent past and the near future. I put in in worded highlights because so many of my friends and family on the European Continent keep saying "We never hear about any of this here". They simply have no inkling of the level of vitriol, unfounded hatred, deeply bigoted dislike and hopeless avoidance of conflict resolution that is directed their way, at their cultures and countries.

Very few Europeans understand the cultural shift that I have lived through, to my own personal and business/financial detriment, in the United Kingdom of Great Britain.

When I arrived in 2013, I was still a relatively welcomed Australian expat, from the former colony of course so easy to patronise by all Brits apparently. When they realised I would not relinquish my German surname due to a marriage with an English farmer, they became passive aggressive in the extreme. All sorts, from every direction.

By 2019, Germans are now Europeans and Britons are not. In fact, when I leave the UK on one my many business trips and escape from the climate of fear, anxiety and hatred, people randomly ask me "Oh so you going to Europe?".

I tell them no, I am already in Europe, standing here with them as European Brits in England. Many of them now refuse to agree, having changed the past in their minds geographically, culturally and historically.

APHORISMS: Part III

Be confident they say, the world is your oyster

Till you crack the shells to find someone's

wearing your pearls

Be yourself at all times is said to be authentic

Women do that and are relegated to lower

echelons of power

Women in business have it tough

Boycotts of the mind are

Worse than purchasing blockades

Discrimination becomes tangible when women speak out, #MeToo was always YouToo, sooner or later.

Inspiration is all important for achievement

Without being inspired we stagnate

To harbour malice is a sign of insecurity

Pity it damages so much of its surrounds

people who are petty

sadly rule some domains of our lives

best to negotiate escape routes early on

ESSAY 3: The Present

I nearly died in Villefranche sur Mer on Monday. I almost gave birth there too, but that is another story, best told in a novella on the life-death cycle at the geographical, cultural and spiritual place where humankind in Europe settled first.

No wonder, the Mediterranean warmth, protection of coastal plains, sea grazing and fecund plains of mammoths. The Grotto du Lazaret hints at the caves of plenty and abundance, security and pleasure in the prehistoric sunshine and milder wintry climes as the Earth heaved and moved inexorably into the shapes we know today.

It had been a stressful technology launch over 5 countries and livestreamed globally. Anything that could go wrong, did go wrong. I was fatigued already the week before, liaising, coercing, persuading, big stick whipping and even having to second guess sabotaging competitors who were out to get David upstarts like us. Go away Goliaths.

Anyway, celebrating the closure of this phase, I missed a step in a medieval stairwell in the Old Town of Villefranche. The startling violence of this fall up a flight of hard rock, unevenly hewn stairs was that I don't recall the sensation of falling. I cracked my skull and the concussion meant little recollection.

What this short essay is about: the signifying power of a black eye on a woman. I thankfully have never had a punch up, a blue and purple swollen face. I have managed to avoid major illnesses, operations, assaults, accidents and the garden variety of mishaps leading victims to hospitals and long recoveries from injury.

Yes I am fortunate and perhaps even one of the Worried Well, though I don't worry that much about my health. Exercise and good diet sure, but not much more than that. Living in the present, as the focus of these few pages suggests, requires that ever popular notion of "mindfulness", a type of default meditative state where you just accept the things that have happened in life, try to deal with the outcomes the best you can and look forward to tomorrow.

"Tomorrow is another day" as the profound statement of my Australian-Irish maternal grandmother would pronounce in her ancient wrinkled wisdom. "Thank God for small mercies", would counter my Catholic Bavarian immigrant paternal grandmother, who was never able to live in the present fully. Much like my other Aussie grandma who was an optimist by comparison though sunk in past recollections.

Having lost memory can be a form of mindfulness I suddenly discovered, lying in the Emergency Ward of the Nice University Hospital Group. I was surrounded by French people were of the same

27

vintage of the aforementioned grandmothers, ancient residents of Nice who had suffered falls and were lying moanfully with bloodied heads and injured limbs.

One of my neighbours might have been a 100 years old, though her sprightly vitality was spurred by a vociferous dementia. It turned out to be a 6 hour long, incessantly loud rendering of any number of characters and dramas going on inside her broken head. It was entertaining at first, the cries of indignation, the dramatic exchanges of these invisible people surrounding her trolley bed near mine, the exhortations in High French and the denouement of conflicts played out mentally in a repeat cycle for decades.

I was wheeled to a side room but could still hear the monologue of this hospitalised amateur actress in her twilight years. It became an extended radio play and improved my French. I picked words and phrases that were expressed emotionally and vividly, casting the scene as brightly as it effervesced in the ill mind of this injured old lady.

"Monsieur, General, Le Maire… " the cast of the imaginary characters of Ancient Nice filled the Emergency Room and the drawn out dialogues and resolving of conflict wafted over the injured, almost healing in the diatribes that ran into the early hours of the morning. Even when the actor was herself wheeled away to a separate room, we could hear her stage voice booming out the door, heedless of walls and nurses' imploring her to be quiet. Not this woman with a black eye.

After several hours of lying in a dazed shock, I stood up. I had a hospital gown on, revealing my naked back behind where the laces had not been tied. I still had my stockings and high heeled boots on. My hair looked like a riotous wig from a pantomime because two days earlier, I decided to dye it from blonde to jet black. Just for fun and to show that women don't need to be fair to have the best fun. Was I preempting fate?

My home hairdo was meant to be fixed by professionals but The Accident on the Medieval Stairs pushed that aside. So I stood at the A&E desk, surrounded by floating beds of The Injured, trying to remember my French which failed me in my mental state. Resorting to English with the patient nurses, I became aware of The Actress agitated behind me.

Seeing me, she had leaped upright to the end of her bed and screamed in the most theatrical fashion a tale about moi. "Arrete la Salope!" she cried. "Stop the whore! Somebody grab the slutty streetwalker and stop the bitch". Uncomfortable silence around me.

I had recognised the Old French word for prostitute from Flaubert's Madame Bovary, or was it the erotic poems of Baudelaire. Didn't matter, I was too dazed to be embarrassed, just amused in a serene, "accepting the state of things" way.

Curiously, when I was returned to the specialist Hospital for the Face & Throat to get my facial wound and fractures checked with a new specialist surgeon, there was a big RED ALERT sign on the entrance. "There could be a terrorist attack here today, please comply with security". The waiting room was accordingly empty. And I was in to see the Dr in no time.

The Present is a time when the one place I would run to so as to escape street roaming terrorists out to massacre the innocent, a hospital, is no longer safe. It has evidently become a target. Like schools in the USA and festivals in most European cities. We are no longer safe in the spaces that usual wartime violence spares.

It changes your perspective on health, safety, security. What can one do, when you wish to live in the present, yet a silly misstep could cause a serious injury to yourself or others?

When all permeating stress, envy and passive aggressive behaviour of others in your everyday life pile up and complicate what should be quite simple matters of life, business and pleasure.

Getting back to the purpose of what my purple, green and black eye in a swollen face has signified in this present week of recovery (taking a lot of pharmaceutical drugs which have helped greatly, thank you French doctors and Western Medicine…):

❑   I looked like a "battered woman" which has been startling for me, dealing with the embarrassed and curious glances thrown my way. How and why was SHE injured? I try to throw back "I am not a victim" look without knowing if it has worked, or whether I must accept being pitied and worried about in the present.

❑   Where I have been living in the Old Town of Nice, Vieux Ville, is owned by the local Catholic Church. Part of St Rita de Cascia's church building, my lovely apartment is on the top floor above the medieval chapel. I find out by accident that St Rita is the Patron Saint of Battered Women, Wives in Abusive Relationships, Illness, Wounds and the Patron Saint of Impossible Causes.

❑   When I walk around the streets and by the sea for fresh air, some men find my black eye arousing. I baulked when I realised the stares at my wounded face were sleazy and inviting me to make contact. Developing Stare #2 "Get Lost!"

❑   This weekend Les Gilets Jaunes Movement were protesting in greater numbers than ever in Nice. Though Paris was the summit of all the discontent. The protests have made me reconsider what France is, where it is going, what happened here in the past to lead to this conflict-driven present. The latest protest is about the Black, Purple, Red, Green, Swollen

Eyes caused by police violence.

❑   This current *Manifestation des blessés*, Protest of the Wounds, focuses on the "fire-ball" anti-riot police weaponry, or the new rubber bullets shot at the demonstrators' faces. I had seen banners and placards in mini demos in the weeks gone by, on the streets, Places, and in the alleys of the Old Town.

❑   Now the new symbol added to the Yellow Vest is the Yellow Eye Patch – worn over the right eye, just like my injury. A truly unexpected signification of it.

I picked up some groceries on Garibaldi Place after seeing a long, free play reading – a new theatre work by a local woman writer - about a pretty young Russian aristocrat and her ménage à trois love affair with Nietsche and some other suitor.

Still mulling over the Russian Roulette dramatic climax at the checkout, my eye injury caught the disdaining gaze of a well-dressed, middle-aged gay couple queuing behind me.

I might have been a Modern Day Salope again. Bending over try-ing to get my crepe ingredients, cheese, soup and non-solid foods from the awkward black basket with a long handle, my black map bag or "writer's satchel" gets caught on the rim and violently tips and pushes the handle into one of the men's crotches.

I see this at eye level, crouched down with the groceries in my embarrassment. Grabbing the out of control plastic trolley bas-ket I can only mutter repeatedly,

"Pardon, Pardon, Pardon Monsieur!" to which I receive an unim-pressed, cold stare of disdain for my clumsiness and the sorry state of my face. To be fair to my accidental injury, it is recovering valiantly and to the best of its ability for now, in the present.

***

Google Maps - my Local Guide "Hit Images"

Google Maps informed me recently that I am "in the top 5% of Local Guides for Nice".

March 2019.

Saint Jean Cap Ferrat

Tania Peitzker

Tania Peitzker

Tania Peitzker

Antibes - my yacht club

Tania Peitzker

Cote d'Azur - Promenade des Anglais

Photos Taken for my ebook Crux - An Addendum.

These pictures are to illustrate the choreography for the play and assist the dancers and musicians in creating the scenes.

The Kindle ebook also includes 3 videos of skateboarders dancing on the promenade and parrots singing in trees between the walkway and street.

Tania Peitzker

Tania Peitzker

Tania Peitzker

Tania Peitzker

Monte Carlo, Monaco

In support of a local woman's group that meets in MC, I posted these pics online to promote the strategic partner hotel...

I can no longer download these photos from Google Maps. Please look them up under my account as a Local Guide: nizzatania@gmail.com Tania Peitzker